good answers
to tough questions

About Dependence
and Separation

Written by Joy Berry

 CHILDRENS PRESS ®

CHICAGO

Managing Editor: Cathy Vertuca
Copy Editor: Annette Gooch
Contributing Editor: James Gough, M.D.

Art Direction: Communication Graphics
Designer: Jennifer Wiezel
Illustration Designer: Bartholomew
Inking Artist: Claudia Brown
Lettering Artist: Linda Hanney
Coloring Artist: Michele Collier
Typography and Production: Communication Graphics

Published by Childrens Press
in cooperation with Living Skills Press

1 2 3 4 5 6 7 8 9 R 98 97 96 95 94 93 92 91 90

This book can answer the following questions:
- How do you become dependent on other people, things, and places?
- Does your dependency change as you become older?
- How does it feel to be separated from the people, things, and places you depend on?
- What facts about separation do you need to know?
- How can you handle separation appropriately?

When you were a baby, you were helpless.

You were not able to protect yourself or provide the things you needed to survive and grow.

You depended on other **people** to keep you safe by protecting you and keeping you from harm.

When you were a baby, you depended on other **people** to meet your physical needs by making sure you had the food, water, clothing, and shelter you needed.

You also depended on them to meet your emotional needs for things such as love and respect.

When you were a baby, you most likely felt safe and secure around the people who took care of you.

When these people were not around—when you were separated from them—you might have felt frightened and insecure.

Besides depending on people, you depended on **things** that made you feel safe and secure.

For example, you might have depended on a special blanket because it kept you warm, and when you nestled under it, you felt that nothing could get to you and hurt you. The blanket might have had an odor that reminded you of the people who loved and took care of you.

You might have felt the same way about a favorite toy or some favorite clothes.

You might also have depended on **things** that helped to meet your needs.

For example, you might have depended on a baby bottle because it held the food and water that you needed. Or you might have depended on a pacifier because, like all babies, you had a need to suck, and the pacifier helped satisfy this need.

When the things you depended on were not around—when you were separated from them—you might have felt frightened.

Being separated from the things you depended on might also have caused you to feel insecure.

In addition to depending on people and things, you depended on **places** that made you feel safe and secure.

You felt protected in those places because you were used to them and you knew what to expect. You knew that nothing harmful would happen to you while you were there.

For example, when you were in your crib or playpen, you probably felt protected. You might have felt the same way about your bedroom and your family's home.

When you were not in the places you depended on—when you were separated from them—you might have felt frightened.

Being separated from the places you depended on might also have made you feel insecure.

Some people think that as a person gets older, he or she becomes totally independent.

Being totally independent means never depending on people, things, or places to protect you or meet your needs.

No one ever becomes totally independent. Everyone, no matter how old he or she is, depends on people, things, and places in one way or another.

Being dependent is a part of being human.

Of course, you will not always depend on the same things in the same way. Your dependence on people, things, and places will change as you grow and change.

For example, when you were a baby, you might have depended on a blanket to make you feel safe. But as you became older and realized your blanket could not protect you, you probably stopped depending on it for protection. Instead, you depended on it to keep you warm.

Another example of how your dependence changes as you grow and change is that when you were a baby, you depended on your parents to feed and dress you. However, as you became older and learned to feed and dress yourself, you probably stopped depending on your parents to do these things for you. Instead, you depended on them to help you do other things, such as make decisions and solve problems.

SO, DO YOU THINK I SHOULD GO OUT FOR SOCCER OR JOIN THE SWIM TEAM?

Some people think that as a person gets older, he or she becomes immune to separation.

Being immune to separation means not being affected by it. It means not being concerned or upset about being separated from a person, thing, or place you are dependent on.

No one ever becomes totally immune to separation. Everyone is dependent on something and is affected when separated from it.

Like other human beings, when you are separated from people you are dependent upon, you might feel
- **afraid** that you might get hurt because they are not around to protect you,
- **angry** that you are separated from them, and
- **insecure** because you do not know what is going to happen to you while they are gone.

You might also feel
- **worried** that something might prevent you from reuniting with them,
- **left** out because you are unable to participate in whatever they are doing, and
- **lonely** because you miss being around them.

These feelings can cause you to lose your appetite or become physically ill.

Like other human beings, when you lose something that you are dependent upon, you might feel
- **frustrated** because you cannot find the object,
- **angry** at yourself or at someone else for losing it, and
- **disappointed** that you will not be able to use the object again.

You might also feel
- **sad** that it is gone, and
- **worried** that you will not be able to replace the lost object.

When you leave a place you are dependent upon, you might feel
- **insecure** because you do not know what is going to happen to you in the new location, and
- **worried** that you won't like being in the new location.

You might also feel
- **sad** that you will be leaving the surroundings that are familiar to you, and
- **overwhelmed** and frustrated because you have to adjust to an entirely new situation.

Separation can cause you to feel uncomfortable. However, knowing some important facts about separation can help you feel better.

Fact #1: Separation is a part of life and cannot be completely avoided.

It is impossible to be around any person, thing, or place all of the time.

For example, you cannot go to work with your parents and they cannot go to school with you. Therefore, you must be separated from them some of the time.

Also, you need to go to school and other important places. Therefore, you must be separated from your home some of the time.

Fact #2: Separation can help you grow and become a better person.

Separation forces you to be without something you are dependent upon. During the separation, you learn that you can survive without the thing you have depended upon. Often, the separation helps you develop better ways to get your needs met.

For example, when you were forced to be separated from your parents, you learned that you could survive without them. You learned to develop relationships with other people, such as your friends and teachers. These new relationships most likely provided better ways to fulfill your social and educational needs.

Fact #3: Separation can help you avoid overdependence.

Overdependence is depending too much on a person, thing, or place.

You are overdependent if your dependence keeps you from doing things that you can and should do for yourself.

For example, you might become so dependent on your parents to make your decisions that you never learn to make decisions for yourself.

Or you might become so dependent on TV for entertainment that you might never develop your creativity or the ability to entertain yourself.

You are overdependent if your dependence on something controls you.

For example, you might become overdependent on a favorite article of clothing and not be able to function normally unless you are wearing it.

Or you might become overdependent on a certain bed and not be able to sleep unless you are in it.

Separating yourself from things can help you overcome your overdependence on them.

Fact #4: Resisting separation can make experiencing it more difficult.

Resisting separation is refusing to accept it or doing everything you can do to stop it from happening.

Resistance takes a lot of time and effort. Sometimes it causes a lot of pain and unhappiness.

For example, some children resist separation from their parents by throwing a tantrum. Often, the tantrum causes the parents to become angry or upset. When this happens, the child is forced to deal with the parents' uncomfortable feelings, as well as the separation.

Resisting separation in this way can cause you to spend unnecessary time, energy, and effort in throwing a tantrum and in dealing with the negative situation the tantrum causes.

Separation from the people, things, and places that you are dependent upon can cause you to feel frightened and insecure. However, separation can also cause you to grow and become a better person if you follow three important steps to handling it appropriately.

Step One: Face the separation.

Acknowledge this fact: the separation is going to happen.

Step Two: Accept the separation.

Accept this fact: There is most likely nothing you can do to stop the separation from happening.

Step Three: Do whatever is necessary to make the separation as easy as possible on everyone.

If you are ever separated from someone you are dependent upon, you can make yourself feel better by doing these things:

Find out
- how long the separation will last (when it will begin and end),
- where you will be and what you will be doing during the separation,
- where the other person will be and what he or she will be doing during the separation,
- how you will be able to contact the person, and
- when and how the person will contact you.

You can get this information by talking to your parents or to the adults who are responsible for you during the separation.

Do whatever you can do to make the separation a positive experience.

- Give the person a pleasant good-bye.
- Keep yourself busy with positive activities during the separation.
- Talk to other people about the person whenever you miss him or her.
- If possible, telephone or write letters to the person.
- Use a calendar to help you keep track of the separation (mark off each day).
- Think about the happy day when you will be getting back together with the person.

If you are temporarily separated from something you are dependent upon, you can make yourself feel better by trying not to focus on the object you are missing.

Instead, find something else to be the focus of your attention. Look for positive features of the objects you have, and try to appreciate and enjoy them.

If you should lose something you are dependent upon, you can make yourself feel better by doing your best to find it.

- Return to where you last saw the object and search for it.
- Make a thorough search of the places where you used the object.
- Ask other people to help you find the object.

If you are unable to find the object, you can make yourself feel better by doing whatever you can to get over the loss.

- Give yourself a specific amount of time to find the object and stop looking for it when the allotted time has passed.
- Figure out whether and how the object can be replaced, and then replace it as soon as possible.
- Try not to focus on the missing object. Instead, think of the things you still have and be thankful for them.

If you are temporarily separated from a place you are dependent upon, you can make yourself feel better by trying not to focus on the place you are missing.

Instead, focus your attention on the place where you are. Look for positive features of the place and try to appreciate and enjoy them.

If you should have to move from a home you have become dependent upon, you can make yourself feel better by learning all you can about your new home and neighborhood *before* you move.

Find out about the
- school you will attend,
- church or synagogue you might attend, and
- community programs and activities available to people your age.

You can learn about your new community by visiting it or by contacting its chamber of commerce for information.

Do whatever you can to make the move go as smoothly as possible.

Do these things before you move:
- Get the addresses and telephone numbers of your special friends and neighbors so you can keep in touch with them.
- Collect photographs and mementos from the community you will be leaving. Store these items in a scrapbook or special box.
- Help your family pack. Be sure to pack your own belongings.

Do these things after you move:
- Unpack your own belongings and set up your own bedroom.
- Make new friends and get involved in your community as soon as possible.
- Concentrate on what you like about the new community.
- Telephone or write letters to your special friends and neighbors from the old community.
- Look at photographs and mementos from the old community.

When dealing with dependence and separation, it is important for you to remember that you have within you the ability to get everything you need to survive and grow.

Being separated from the things you depend on can cause you to become more independent.

As you become more independent, you will most likely become a happier, healthier, more productive person.